Peace in the Midst of the Storm

Peace in the Midst of the Storm

Kaleb Thompson

RESOURCE *Publications* · Eugene, Oregon

PEACE IN THE MIDST OF THE STORM

Resource Publications
An Imprint of Wipf and Stock Publishers
199 W. 8th Ave., Suite 3
Eugene, OR 97401

www.wipfandstock.com

PAPERBACK ISBN: 978-1-6667-3399-0
HARDCOVER ISBN: 978-1-6667-2937-5
EBOOK ISBN: 978-1-6667-2938-2

11/08/21

Cover Art: Ryan Lause (courtesy of 99Designs)

For the unsettled
For the powerless
For the hurting
For the restless

For the strong-willed
For the changed and the healed
For the tenacious
For the secure

For the optimistic
For the spontaneous
For the thriving
For the free

This is for you.

Peace I leave with you; My peace I give you. I do not give to you as the world gives. Do not let your hearts be troubled and do not be afraid.

—John 14:27

Contents

Acknowledgements

I WOULD FIRST LOVE to extend my sincere gratitude to my Lord and my Savior Jesus Christ in providing me the strength and the motivation to create such a promising poetry book that I believe will inspire others. Therefore, this is such a beautiful blessing to share pieces of my story as well as using my voice and my words to help uplift, guide, and empower the brokenhearted, yet the spiritually grounded. There were times when self-doubt and anxiety attempted to slow me down, but I am extremely grateful that I never lost sight in remaining dedicated towards completing a significant piece of work that will forever be valuable to me. The confidence that I have gained in making sure this book comes to life would not have been possible without the comfort and hope that I have received from the both of you. Once again, I give my thanks for bringing me to this point of my life filled with endless possibilities. My faith and trust remain committed to honoring the both of you.

I would also love to mention my humble family, consisting of my loving parents and my gracious siblings who have shown their consistent support in making sure my specific goal of publishing this poetry book would be accomplished. All of you encourage me to be my best self and continue to inspire me by enabling me to see how a great work ethic and self-value brings forth a prosperous life. The passion that I felt throughout this fundamental, yet tedious process elevated me to make all of you prouder even more. With that said, I am greatly blessed that I have been given a tight-knit family that values generosity, harmony, resilience, growth, and positivity. To my parents, I thank you for your active listening and patient understanding in hearing and reading my reflections of joy and sorrow. To my siblings, your grit and optimism never made room for me to give up. What I intended to start, I did intend to finish due to all of you believing in me. I love all of you with every breath in me.

Acknowledgements

To my very supportive friends who I have been blessed to have, I will forever appreciate the gracious advice and the willingness that each of you show in enabling me to persevere throughout my good and my bad days. Thank you for faithfully believing in me, even though there were plenty of times that I failed to believe in myself. I pray that we never lose sight on what we were placed in this world to do and that we continue to uplift one another. Let us continue to enjoy this uncertain, yet beautiful life together.

Introduction

WHEN THE STORM IN your life is raging, remember that it will not last always. This life wasn't promised to be easy for all of us, but we were graced with the vital strength to endure through even the most difficult challenges. Therefore, the inner peace within you will encourage you to hold on and never give into defeat as your divine breakthrough will begin to manifest in the blink of an eye. If you're hurting, it's only temporary. If you're feeling alone, it's only temporary. Constricted in fatigue and restlessness, it's only temporary. What you have started out in becoming will only lead to a valuable transformation where you will no longer be anxious about anything. Hope hears your strained voice as love willingly comforts to make your broken spirit whole. Time enables you to hold yourself accountable for your own happiness. Your seed will sprout into rejuvenation for your tomorrow and the days ahead. I pray you heal from your past, embrace what you have now, and honor the need of choosing yourself as well as prepare for a beautiful future that nourishes and completes your soul.

Faith, resilience, empowerment. The beauty of faith transitions us as troubled individuals into calm-spirited souls as we are at rest knowing that everything will work together for our good. Faith is the substance of things hoped for and the evidence of things that are unseen. What has been positioned to bring us deserving favor, whether it be a promising career or unexpected financial well-being, is a valuable gift that is not at risk of being taken away. Through the difficult storm, faith enables us to possess clearer vision beyond what others do not have the desire to see themselves. As we embrace the light that has lifted us from where darkness has placed us, we are courageous enough to become resilient in pushing ourselves to be redefined as meek and worthy. We are too involved in pursuing our designated purpose that we have become disinterested in looking back to what we once were. We are no longer the same as we refuse to let what was meant to break us affect our mental, physical, and spiritual mentality. I can only imagine how proud we must be to bury distraught and worry and secure the value of expressing the confidence to overcome anything. Therefore, this is where empowerment lies. Empowerment grants us the necessity of giving ourselves the permission to be steadfast in focusing on where we need to go and where we need to be. We were built to heal and elevate from the scars that attempted to permanently damage our sacred temples. We were built to stand firmly, in spite of the obstacles that were repeatedly present. We were built to know that we are enough.

The storms that were created to deter us into a state of depression, hurt, pain, and fear were actually meant to provide strength, a true asset most of us never knew we had. Justified by growth, we have now realized that we are immune to brokenness and are willing to survive from the bondage of negativity. The spirit of discernment is also a key factor towards how our storms can easily dissipate within our lives as the people that are placed around us should be given heavy consideration in terms of their investment within our lives. The people who remain dedicated in growing with us desire to honor commitment and loyalty, resulting in us being at peace with ourselves and simply embracing our storms, knowing that they will wash away. It also begins within us to position ourselves into our manifestation. We must be able to withstand the test, no matter how difficult it may be, for patience and positivity will truly reward us with abundant blessings as the gray clouds disappear and the sun smiles directly on us. We all have been through something, some of us are going through something, but we must adhere to the fact that we have to endure in order to become better than what we originally were. My personal testament of dealing with anxiety, fear, doubt, and hurt are specific issues that I've had to reflect within myself in order to grow boldly in spirit. By the grace of God, I am situated in positive thoughts, healthy well-being, and self-love, which I am very grateful for.

We have to encourage ourselves. The obstacles that we are facing, we have to press through them. The guilt that we have accumulated from our past, we have to let it go. The people who were only meant to be present for a season, we have to let them go, as they were not equipped to accompany us on our journey of fulfillment. It may feel rough being alone, especially when our storms are becoming more aggressive, but that only exudes the strength to come out of them and embrace the better days that will always be ahead. We will make it. We will conquer what was attempting to keep us down. It's time to wipe our tears, move forward in gratitude, and hold ourselves to living in peace.

Going Through

Another day has passed and here I am once more
Patiently waiting on the precise moment when self-destruction succumbs to true happiness
Transitioning into a new life that breathes immense passion and newfound freedom that my well-being will adore
I want to be exalted into a meaningful place that dignifies genuine love instead of a harrowing emptiness

Excuse me for expressing how I truly feel
I am not well as my heart and my soul quietly ache
It's so difficult to continue to live with such unstable pain that I desperately want to be unreal
I am this close to throwing in the towel because of the unmovable demons of doubt and brokenness that seem too stagnant to shake

This state of motionless grief that I am heavily consumed in has therefore left me speechless
Bottled up inside a contaminated mind, just realize that I am only going through
The settled darkness has polluted my inability to saturate in the welcoming light, leaving me an undesirable mess
Feeling blue and feeding negative energy in a decaying soul like a rotten honeydew

No need to worry . . . for the phase I am in is only temporary
Once again, I am only going through
The joy and happiness that I thrive for in life are what my heart longs to carry
Transcending into a comforting place of serenity will be a hopeful journey that my life will soon leap into

Lord, Remember Me

As I self-reflect on life's difficult challenges and bountiful blessings
Being stricken with anxiety yet embracing divine prayer
Your evident grace and mercy has strengthened me to keep pressing
Father God, you've done more than enough as my wonderful counselor and
waymaker

Falling short of meeting your expectations because of easy temptations
Disappointment often ensued as I turned my life astray from you
Realizing that Heaven is what I long for, following the loving example of
Christ comes with much dedication
Father God, as I claim you as my Savior with a sincere heart, my life in your
hands has become greatly anew

Your still, small voice strengthens my ability to achieve my aspirations in
life, while remaining spiritually intact
With the mistakes I have made, you still love me and continue to smile
down on me as I can see
All of my help comes from you as a matter of fact
As time never ceases, Lord please remember me

I'm at peace knowing you will never leave me nor forsake me
For your spirit will remain in me forever and a day
My life will continue to pour out unto thee
Your presence and protection will always manifest without delay

Lord, remember me as I have fallen short of your glory
Renew my mind to embrace confidence instead of constant worry
From a pastor's son, a child of you I will always be
Lord, please just remember me as my purpose is to be with you for eternity

Forgiven

Many times I disobeyed
Sometimes I intentionally did wrongful things
Rarely did I want to take responsibility for my nonchalant behavior

Father God, thank you for never giving up on me
As I have continued to ask for your desire to receive second chances
I know I'm not perfect but being more like you is all that I require to be
Loving myself and others is what I will always stand by as a beneficial stance

I choose to live the rest of my life in peace
Through my battles and mistakes, I'm forgiven
I know better so I'm doing better by putting childish things to a cease
The old me has washed away; maturity I was indeed given

When You Pray

The instant freedom
The lasting sensation
Your heart gradually placed back whole
The feeling of being consoled

When you pray, doesn't your worries suddenly go away?
The end result being a dignified praise that you now carry with you each day
You are restored, resting with your mind and soul in quiet solitude
Nothing is sweeter than a private interlude that creates a wonderful change
in sustaining a positive mood

When you pray, the Lord is working on your behalf
The best is yet to come
Stand in monumental faith as the miracles fall and the angels harmoniously
hum
Stand in spiritual justice for your prayers will be answered in due time

When you pray, the relationship you build with the Lord is complete
You feel the urge to talk to him about anything, especially when you believe
you have no one else to talk to
The everlasting joy you will spread, the worry that you will beat
Think of the love that the Lord has always had and will continue to have
for you

Pray with conviction
Pray with action
Always remember to pray on your good and rough days
For when you pray, you will be at rest

Amen

Dear Lord,

Another glorious day has come and I pray that we continue to be more like you
We should not become discouraged when our obstacles attempt to overpower us as your grace and mercy has always brought us through
Help us to be grateful for the small things
For breath in our bodies and sincere happiness supports what the meaning of life divinely brings

I pray that we will all see the bigger picture
Let us not remain comfortable where we easily stand
We have so much more to give; it is our true passion that brings us great rapture
Help us achieve prolonged success that will remain unmoved on our names, our legacies, and our brands

I'm asking you to hold our hands to guide us every step of the way
Place your footprints on our direct paths as we walk towards what you need us to be
May our positive emotions not be shifted by the misty skies presented to us dull and gray
Open our eyes to explore our dreams that you have set into reality

Lord, remind us to remember you
It's so disheartening to forget you as we know we're not perfect
We can be our own hypocrites and these are definitely some hard words to chew
As we feel the need to sin, may your voice come through and intersect

I thank you for being who you are
Without you, we would be nothing
Your guiding light and seamless love have brought us this far
Lord, thank you for simply being our everything

In Jesus name that I pray,

Amen!

The Revival

Our old, crooked ways have freely departed from us
We're no longer tamed to what we were in the past
Our toxic emotions have been cremated, where the ashes have passed away
into the sea of forgetfulness
How sweet it is to make a conscious decision to celebrate new life

Grooming positive thoughts and actions
Nurturing spiritual health
Changing ourselves into more polished brands of what we should aspire
to be
The value of growth, what one sees as a ultimate victory

We had to want and do better for ourselves
To elevate and not to hinder
To rise and not to fall
To serve and not to be selfish

We have finally accepted ourselves as grown adults
Childish mentalities left behind
Simple-minded thoughts suddenly lost in plain sight
We have been revived

Armed in mercy
Forgiveness that was shared
The jury acquitted us from a life in utter disrepair
Shame we no longer feel as we have been revived into greater beings

Rise

What you speak into existence is the summary of everything you wrote
Just be mindful your tongue does not lash out what you will later regret
When the Sun comes up, take a good look
Only in darkness you won't stay long; the next day, you will rise

Your scars will heal
Inevitable strength that your soul will gain
Your feelings won't be entrapped by hurtful judgements
Delivered from the subjected pain your inner demons caused when you assumed your life was in vain
You're no longer insane
For the baggage that was once chained to your mind has been removed
The day you embrace when you will reap tears of joy because you have decided to rise

Your demeanor reflects insecurities
Untapped potential because of your unhealthy habit to compare
Grant yourself the aspect of obtaining truthful courage and rightful liberty
Remember, the Lord made you perfect in his image; he'll never put more on you than you can bear

You pass away slowly like a leaf dissected from its branch
Withering away with the grass
Stained with the mud and the dirt that has accumulated your present life
Oh how wonderful it is when you plant your seed of faith on the brink of giving up
Just as soon as the rain floods necessary abundance will you rise as proud as a beautiful sunflower

Your manifestation awaits you

The endearing future that you couldn't see is now embodied into your destiny

You no longer settle for less, your obstacles decompressed, a table you have built where your enemies have become your guests

See how quick the tables have turned

You rose above the madness

The prideful opinions masqueraded as distracted noises

All because you continue to fly high instead of waiting to die

Let Your Light Shine

Aren't you proud of yourself?
Radiating with such positive energy and beaming with perfect health
Those around you astonished, wrongfully contemplating that you would stumble and fall with nothing left
Instead, they feel ashamed because of how you openly emerged with great wealth

Others mistreated you with bruised intentions, you forgave them
Your name was mentioned in foolish gossip, you ignored it
You have the last laugh because of your desire to let your light shine, instead of letting it dim
Your presence only disturbed their stubborn hearts because of your remarkable wit

You gained true respect and lost self-pity
You went through the fire only to be extinguished with grace
You speak and walk with divine favor that inspires plenty
An open heart many love to embrace

I gasp at the self-righteous despising your worth
For they are ignorant of your trying, yet incredible journey
Held back by their insecurities, you maintain the urge to move forth
Continue to unlock amazing opportunities with your humble spirit, you hold the master key

You won
You are handling the world just fine
So much more you have to accomplish as your work is not done
With a conqueror's cry, let your light shine!

I Am Not The World

What society worships, I condemn
The entitled are placed on a high pedestal, instead of the generous and selfless
Drama appears to be more of a hopeless gem
Class and sophistication seem to be so far gone

The world will attempt to conform you into doing things that I know I
wasn't raised to do
I was taught to give respect for good things will gravitate towards me
doublefold
I pray some will adapt to this mentality as we all need a helping hand to hold
For a better place the world will be when we all come together

I desire to walk free in my own right
Controlling my independence and minding my own business
I've subscribed towards creating my own path instead of quickly following
behind others
As I know that my peace will be guarded

It's a scary feeling how we come to realize that this world has been going
backwards
Equality and equity are rarely existent
We tear each other down more than ever
Modeling disloyalty and turmoil continue to be the norms society adheres to

I am changed into the man that I have grown to be
I am not persuaded to be a reproductive copy of anyone else
I will never devalue myself to what the world remains standardized to
I am what I am; I am not the world

The Boy Who Never Frowns

Keeping a smile in this bitter world seems so hard to do
But when love and peace overpower pain and guilt, no underlying issue will ever tremble the soul
Continue to embody the essence of a guiding light, shining very bright and inspiring others, even if only a few
In this world where desperation and negativity seem to reign, we need to be made whole

Being raised to always appreciate the smallest things
Positivity is a true gem that will never go unrecognized
Waking up every day to simply enjoy the richest blessings that life truly brings
There rises a giddy feeling when true happiness often leaves one mesmerized

Who am I? I am the boy that never frowns
This joy that I have, the world can't take it away
You see, the Lord created a natural-born king that never tilts his crown
Embracing every beautiful person with a gracious heart that will never decay

Through the storm and through the rain, I smile
Every obstacle that I face is just one step closer to a breakthrough
A life of gratitude I will always cherish as I refuse to live a life unnecessarily vile
Remaining kind and letting my light shine will always be my point of view

Issues at stake, but know to never concede
As kings and queens, remember to never tilt your crowns
Listen carefully as I plead
Again, I say, I am the boy who never frowns

Love Yourself (Cause The World Don't)

Born masterfully to endure, you have true purpose
Intended to value self-respect and dismiss low self-esteem
Uniquely placed in a dark world where your sparkling light gleams
Sustained confidence where your self-worth will not diminish will never run you off course

In a world where integrity is often compromised, do not lose yourself
For greater is in store for ones who continue to live right
This world, with so much chaos and confusion, entails problematic pressures and constant battles to fight
Secure your inner and outer peace with all your might

Appreciate self-love as people who demean you are only jealous souls
Don't you know that others value you more six feet under, lying there to rot
Remain true for your sanity as giving yourself to corruption only digs deeper holes
Therefore, love yourself completely because truth be told, the world does not

The Devil Strikes (When You're Closer To God)

Baptized and freed into a hallow soul so fresh and mature
The relationship that I have with my God is personal and pure
I insanely laugh in the face of the Devil
Knowing that he will never reach the Lord's level

It must be so uncomfortable to desire a humble and peaceful spirit more
I know he can't help it for my life has never been the same
The closer that I am with my Father, the more that he loves to play tug-of-war
Satan, how old are you? . . . because I do not participate in childish games

My heart is secured as I ignore the wrath of the Devil
Sin, you deliver; righteousness, you despise
You smile when I struggle, satisfied when I fail but I refuse to stoop to your level
As you are willingly and deservingly chastised

Do not fall for everything for even angels on Earth can drip with iniquity
The more you are exposed to the tricks of the enemy, the more you stray away from doing what is morally right
Submitting yourself to him subjects to absolute pity
Secluded in darkness facing persuasive demons in an unfortunate plight

Joy, peace, love, and meekness clothed through the armor of God
All because you chose to be closer to the most High
You will no longer fall victim to blind and coercive leadership, regardless of what the Devil continues to try
Misery, you will lose and generosity, you will gain as your well will never run dry

I've Learned To Accept My Mistakes

Sin consistently seeped into me
Sincere prayer set me free
A new life has been invested with a positive outlook where I no longer feel
captive to where I have been
For my past has been repressed and forgiven

Careless mishaps molded into careful observations
Untimely failure transforming into valuable success
Second chances arising from unfulfilled declarations
A beautiful future where miraculous blessings will divinely fall into place
I know to expect nothing less

The confidence that was granted through enduring harsh obstacles
The vital lessons that were groomed through the many horrible decisions
that my life has had to take
The better person that I have become through the instant changes that I
had to make
All because of simply learning to accept my mistakes

Success In My Name

I thank the Good Lord for blessing me with a righteous mind
For anxiety dwindles in my presence
No longer does my faith and fear ineffectively bind
Experiencing much-needed growth in living a peaceful life that brings complete essence

Generational sacrifices, dignified effort
Youthful wisdom, acquired respect
Spiritual warfare, divine intervention
Disciplined decisions, favored position

Filled with hope instead of lingering sorrow, now my today urges for tomorrow
For my name will be written above what the sky limits
The power of my conquering spirit will speak volumes that no envious human being will borrow
My mouth shall never utter defeat as success will remain unchanged in a life deemed so precious and fit

Jealous Souls

Wolves in sheep's clothing
Congratulate you publicly yet hate you privately
Criticize and dehumanize as an excuse for remaining motionless in their
own lives like a timid bird who doesn't know how to use its wings
May you quietly accomplish every aspiration and let your success truly ring

Strangers with demented spirits, not knowing the envy some of your family
and friends calmly hide
Claim to be supportive and proud
Disrupted by the realm of emotional distress similar to the moon forcibly
controlling the ocean tides
You could never tell how much they lied

I hope you can abide by this spoken word
If my ambitious drive offends you, either make yourself better or continue
to watch
A jealous soul coated with greed and manipulation cannot breed success
moving forward
*Sincerely, an unbothered individual whose life will continue to overflow with
great reward*

From My Heart To Yours

I sympathize with you
Feeling hopeless and having no sense of direction
Remaining stagnant through life's pivotal trials after all you've been through
What follows is the dismay of personal failure and imminent rejection

I empathize with you
Losing a close family member or friend
Emotionally and physically drained in knowing there was nothing else you could do
Lord, please give us the vital strength in helping our broken hearts to mend

A genuine heart you will allow others to receive
True kindness and respect will never waver
You will never be in vain being a beacon of light in this dark world, best believe
This is sound advice to keep with you always, not just a simple favor

Be grateful for the life that you are living
You were created for a purpose and set to pursue a distinct vision
Remain consistent in being a person so nurturing and giving
In terms of governing your own success, embrace the best decisions

From my heart to yours, I love you
Invest in your inner peace and be enriched by the joy of others
Surround yourself with people who value your presence but never forget to love yourself too
From my heart to yours, be wholesome in sustaining a fruitful life my sisters and brothers

Strength is Power

Slipping and falling on a weary road where your mentality falls victim to subconscious lies
Experiencing the devastating losses of loved ones who you knew passed away too soon
Embracing failure after failure when you remain very close in touching the rim of success, no matter the amount of tries
Ever wonder why you tend to recover from your disappointments and become consistently resilient in overcoming your battles? You have indescribable strength

Kindness should never be taken for granted
For people are easily misinformed that weakness stems from such a powerful emotion
The spirit of discernment is more prevalent these days as we focus on the ones who truly value our presence
Therefore, we no longer dwell in the surroundings of the pretenders as we have been emancipated

The comforting feeling that overflows when your inner wealth is protected
You have true strength
The moment when you openly accept faith into your heart to overcome anything
You have spiritual strength

Allow yourself permission to be placed first
For pure strength is what you have longed to thirst
Imminent power is now written in your story
As you have the ability to change the circumstances that choose to reign over your life

A different person that you have now become
You are courageous enough to travel down that narrow path instead of quickly taking the usual shortcuts
The power of your being rises within you
If only you take the first step to influence the world to be still in gravitating towards the magnitude of strength

For Richer and Not For Poorer

When you wake up in the morning, do yourself a favor and look around
I hope you realize that you were fit to see another day
Your family is still here, your health remains intact, the people you care about are still here
Know that you're blessed, in spite of each day that you had to shed a tear

Note that money isn't everything
For true happiness should be the most honorable thing
You have what you need as what you desire will come to pass
Material things drift away, but spiritual wholeness will always last

Never claim to be poor or destitute, for you are rich in spirit
Life can be riveting, but it gives you the power to navigate your own course
Growth is situated through your mentality
When you speak and act on good things, your reality of self will be so much easier to see

Hope sets in
It's critical to love your life and not complain
Invite your passions and bury the inhibitions
Your spirit will continue to rise from within

You're still living
Make every moment count
Remember that you're special and that you're needed
You're rich because you choose to embrace gratitude, that's what life is about

Life's Journey

Success is not given, it is earned
Through life's choices from which we have learned
Believe in yourself and follow your dream
It's not as hard as it may seem

Friends As These

In a society so fragile, the company you keep may not have your best interest at heart
You give yourself so freely but your friends never offer the same in return
Don't tell yourself that you're not good enough; the Good Lord's only telling you it's time to grow apart
It was for your own good; please refrain from expressing any concern

I was in your shoes; Helped in any way I could but ended up being used
Smiling in my face but talking about me behind my back
I soon realized I had to remove myself altogether, instead of forever living my life emotionally abused
Waiting for God to bless me with the right friends in order to keep myself on track

During my college journey, I was blessed to be enriched with the right people in my life
My friends who continue to motivate me, uplift me, pray for me . . . they get the hint
To become a better me, I had to distance myself from the superficial attitudes and unnecessary strife
To say that I have great friends is truly an understatement . . . they are simply God-sent

So, I encourage you to be of good faith and courage to people who value your present and your future
Friends as these who God has blessed you with shall claim victory and unwavering favor over your life
No longer will negativity plague your spirit as positivity will shower newfound joy and peace, that's for sure
This day forward, be strengthened by your friends as these as you had so much pain and hurt to endure

Open your heart to trust the people who have been placed to help you grow; you will never walk alone
Genuine hearts and precious souls that will sincerely put you at ease
Your overall life has been shifted to embrace greater and to realize that the hurtful past is now gone
Move forward as you have been blessed to have friends as these

Fond Of You

Raising a generation of strong-willed, independent kings and queens
Working to make a living with so little but the foundation of faith and love
was all you ever needed to get by
Nurturing sharp-tongued wisdom to last a lifetime, being a helpful shoulder
that deserves much leaning
Rejoicing, for your children have made something of themselves and have
gained the courage to willingly fly

That gentle smile fixated on your beautiful melanated skin
The warm hugs squeezed so tightly you never want to let go
Indescribable excitement your loved ones feel in your presence, especially
when you have never given up through the thick and thin
And let's not forget the decadent, home-cooked meals and delectable
desserts made freshly homemade and so mellow

You've inspired, uplifted, amazed, and valued so many, even strangers who
you claim as your own
I give you thanks for showing how a true legacy should be remembered
Your sweet spirit and gentle, healing touch are your finest attributes that
will forever be known
Happiness you always saw, positive remarks you always heard

Each day you are here brings everlasting paradise
For you continue living a life so full and rich
Sacrificing yourself for others, you never had to think about twice
You will always be loved because of your shining personality deemed so
lovable and nice

Love, Family

Togetherness instead of brokenness
Jubilance instead of misery
Meekness instead of hopelessness
Forgiveness instead of a broken history

The beauty of a tight-knit family never growing apart
The contagious smiles and encouraging words that bring forth imminent
healing like powerful medicine
Perfectly singing with beautiful melodies and lasting harmonies will forever
be a work of art
Loving personalities so infectious that it completes others from within

Celebrate the living, honor the deceased
We sow positive seeds for our children to reap, through what we learn from
our elders
The needed help and the unfiltered truth will always be leased
I think of my 95 year-old grandmother who is here to witness the knowledge
of spiritual fulfillment that she has instilled through generations
Look at how proud we made her

The unbreakable relationships that foster loyal commitment
How necessary it is for their undying support to remain the same through
ample achievements and dreadful downfalls
Deep love remains rooted when you do everything in your power to care
for your own, regardless of how far our back is bent
Through it all, family will be there when you call

Related through bloodline, our last names are permanently signed
In their hearts is where you'll always be, in their arms is where you can be free
Our souls knowingly align showing an emotion so joyous and benign
We grace our love for eternity; that's simply family

He's O.K.

August 11th, 2017

The day you stepped on that football field brought a surprising revelation that none of us would have seen

Who would've thought your college football journey would be sidetracked by a full-blown concussion?

38 days with the ugly truth admitting that you were only existing . . . as a mere repercussion

I could not even imagine how that weekend felt when a heavy bump to the head would diminish your memory

You were slowly losing yourself; we did not want to assume the worst

Oh how emotional we felt when you could not even grasp the presence of your loving family; the blank stare that soon came to be

We had to understand that this happened for a reason and we had to remain incredibly strong, for it was you we had to put first

You took a temporary detour from your collegiate journey; it was time to come home

Those weary days when you felt depressed and alone at the unsettling thought of not remembering anyone

We couldn't let you give up; we had to stay positive in order for you to remarkably glow like the value of chrome

Remember my little brother, you were healing through your pain

This battle you were fighting had to be won

I saw your struggle; your negative thoughts gave you much ridicule

Your evident body language was enough for us to see

My God, please perform a miracle

My brother just wants to be free

September 19th, 2017

Our fervent prayers came to pass as you rose from a riveting, lengthy nightmare

How relieved your family and close friends were on this day that the Lord nurtured you with tender care

You won this battle, relinquished from this devastating scare

Your college journey has resumed, excelling as an ambitious student-athlete

Overcoming that perilous ordeal, you're ok

The desired aspirations that you have set for yourself, your soul is so dedicated to complete

My brother, you're still here, sewing inspiration and resilience into your legacy where it is meant to stay

Love Ain't

Absorbed as a tactic of healing, yet dismembered from the souls of the depressed and brokenhearted
A deeper feeling that transcends over the grotesque realm of hate
True emotion that gives honor to every life once departed
Expressed freely, helping to foreshadow a meaningful destiny and I hope, favorable fate

Love does not belittle, devour, instigate, or envy
It tastefully remains truthful, sufficient, inevitable, and sustainable
With the disrespect and deceit that we continue to show to each other, an outpour of love desires to be our welcoming plea
Love, a persuasive force that will never lose its ability to be attainable

Using people for your own advantage ain't love
Abuse of any kind ain't love
Self-pity and emotional distress ain't love
Somebody, please detach yourself from the strained relationship of needless hate and foolish love

Love is cherished and bound
A feeling never lost but easily found
Knowingly sure and defiant to being faint
Love ain't meant to end, it just ain't

Heavenly Shadow

I feel your spiritual presence, cherished memories remembering your essence, leaving here suddenly sure left us speechless but your transition made perfect sense
The battle you fought was won and the race you partook in was gracefully completed
Another angel was chosen; no need to tirelessly be included with a world deemed so shallow and dense
Our minds have processed that you are no longer with us, but with our hearts, you will never be deleted

Your angelic spirit exudes harmony and protection
No longer imperfect and your silent, heroic guidance carries us into a sacred place of compassion
Honoring your humble legacy helps lead our family in a profound direction
Your valued time in this world and the life that you now live for eternally will continue to be discussed with so much passion

You are missed, but not forgotten
Physically unseen, but spiritually birthed
Perfect in all your ways, delivered from all of your sins
For you to be settled in an eternal place of serenity, we just knew that you had so much worth

You are our reminder of how much you are still needed
You had to let us know you're still here with us through the constant visit of your heavenly shadow
We were excited that you became situated in a better place but our hearts still grieved heavy, which is one thing you greatly heeded
To be absent in the body is to be present with the Lord—a saying that encourages our family to peacefully grow

Too proud to have had you as our loved one
Your heavenly shadow symbolizes the unwavering love and generosity that you graciously gave us
How your presence used to brighten up the lives of others as compared to the light of the sun
We will always love you
Being a true asset in our family was definitely an ultimate plus

Angels on Earth

Just when I was about to give up on this life
As I thought nothing was going right
Just when my toughest days were getting more weary
As darkness remained there in sight
Angels on this Earth intervened on my behalf

The sleepless nights
The streams of tears that flowed
The aching of my soul and mind
The feeling of weakness that I have known
I have regained my strength because of the angels on Earth who prayed for
me

I feel secure
I no longer feel broken
A radiant smile I proudly show
Another chance to live in glory, a rewarding token
With this, I express gratitude to the angels on Earth who made me whole

Eager to set a positive example
Passionate in denouncing negativity of any kind
A better tomorrow set to be delivered
Rare gems so pleasing to find
How relieving it is to have angels on Earth invested in cleansing this world
with unity and love

I leave behind my self-pity
It's a new day to let it all go
Frustrations deepened my void, yet it makes all the difference when I am
motivated to forget the bad
Here awaits a positive flow as I gave myself permission to grow
The result caused by the angels on this Earth who had me on their minds to
elevate into the blue skies

The Smallest Things

I hope each day allows you to be mindful of what you have
Peace of mind
Impeccable health ·
A forgiving heart, especially when you have chosen to own a wholesome
life justified through optimism and worth

A diamond-studded circle of true friends who celebrate your presence; an
irreplaceable void that is felt when your absence is noticed
A touch from the most High to see a new day
Tenacious strength to persevere
Grace and mercy that saw fit to gift you with a second chance

The warm embrace from family
The warm greeting from a stranger
Prolific words and heartfelt actions showcasing how much you're loved
The beautiful growth you've experienced in loving yourself

A self-fulfilling career that adores your true passion
Your children with their joyous pride, knowing how determined they are to
be a rich reflection of you
Your parents are still charming this Earth with their grace, daily praising
you of how proud they are
You have a humble spirit, never let it deflect from such a good heart

You breathe life and not death
You see beyond the scope as material things and wealth do not take favor
over your soul
You are what the world, I sincerely hope, transforms to desperately be
You're happy to be happy, that's what matters

Easy

Hard is not an option
I'll figure it out the best way I can
As long as I never give up, success will never bother to leave me
On optimism and confidence I stand

Reset, prepare, act
My mind has to reset in order to solely focus on my aspirations
An unafraid mentality, one that will prepare me to honor my wins and accept my losses
I can speak and think of my future as gladly as I please but will not gain anything if I don't act on my desired plans

Stronger I will be when my fears are invalid
The time that won't be wasted being frantic in taking that first step
Changed I will be when my challenges will not define me
The way I move forward and don't look back while adversity fails to rear its ugly head . . . a feeling so adequate

Nothing is ever given, but rightfully earned
Shortcuts are not meant to be taken for the ones who remain poised in endurance and humility
For uncompromised integrity and a diligent work ethic are true concepts that will provide significant importance
Through this will God's grace and favor be evidently attracted to

I can sleep real good, knowing I will overcome anything
For life will be so much easier to withstand
Thank you Lord for your comforting touch; the troubles of this world no longer scare me
And I am grateful to say that I am not afraid

Patience

Success does not happen overnight
Your dreams are planted where your vision will blossom in due season
Your presence was carefully designed to impact this world for a beneficial reason
By faith and your good works, your life has breathed light, and you have already won

The overflow of blessings you have received because you decided not to act too soon
You have a characteristic many find appreciative yet are found in very few
Everything happens for a reason which is why everything falls into place when it's your time
That's why patience is defined as such a virtue

You wait, knowing your dreams and aspirations will align perfectly
What you have planned for a successful life was never intended to be rushed
The peace you will gain when time permits reality to reward you with what you desired to be
For impatience only hinders the miserable and the anxious

The breakthrough that was in store, you were willing to wait
Standing in righteousness empowered you to not extend an invitation to the negative hand of fate
You know that through God, he delivers his promises at the right time as there is never a moment when he comes late
Therefore, may serenity remain infiltrated in such a positive mind state

Your time has come

Embrace what you have been patiently waiting for

Favor will consistently shower upon your life as not one man can put asunder the manifestation of your destiny

Walk in what God has blessed you to achieve on your journey as every chapter lies an open door

Breathe

Close your eyes
Relax and meditate
Unravel the delayed confidence from the hurtful thoughts that's brought
forth aggravating headaches
Collect your inner peace from the calming aura of the sky
Only then will you be authorized to let it all go

Trouble may hinder you, but it's never positioned to stay
Depression is joy's worst enemy, but through time, that joy will come
around and won't be turned loose
Fear imposes on the meek, but when hope is regained, fear will no longer
possess control
Adversity might cause you to stumble, but your strength to endure will
allow you to walk straight

Hold on and remain focused
Setbacks only last for a season
You're gonna make it
You've come too far to fall behind

Inhale positive energy as you exhale the heavy load
See, now your shoulders can also relax
Don't rush this experience as you should expect so much in return
Take the time to be your best self

Instill the courage to leap over your obstacles
Come into agreement that you have power over your situations
Cover yourself to not be easily shaken
Be still and detach yourself from panic
Breathe

Sick

Constant sneezing
Runny nose that seems to never end
Abrupt coughing
We've all experienced these symptoms of the common cold

As you become older, please keep your health and wellness foremost
Take it from me, as I am currently learning
I'm only 23 but I was too docile to the sickening issue of stress
I know life is too short but I want to live with as much longevity as I can

Sinuses and allergies affecting me since a very young age
Chest pains at 20
Hives at 22, an on-and-off relationship
The two latter being life-changing experiences that positively altered the direction of my life
To think I would be exposed to chest pains during my junior year of college and hives a few months into my full-time job . . . utterly speechless

Your body will thank you as you take great care of it
Feeling energized instead of slumped
Being consciously healthy
A temple that you are preserving greatly

Your health remains intact to your physical and spiritual wealth
If you're sick of the detriment effect your career is having on you, leave and value your own worth
If you're sick of being taken advantage of for the last time, distance yourself from those lukewarm individuals
If you're sick of complaining of things beyond your control, give it all to God as he will bring you through

We have been healed from the situations that threatened to take a devastating toll on us
We're soldiers, marching on our own freedom roads, tired of succumbing to unhealthy distractions
Each day we live to see, we're destined to be better
We're no longer sick, we're indebted to change

Talking To Myself

Besides the Good Lord above, I have complete trust in myself
Why do I need to apologize for what others dictate as strange?
I am my own person so don't be disturbed when I engage in self-served conversations; I won't ever change
My best decisions seem to come from my final say, instead of relying on the thoughts and words of others

I am my own friend
For my ability to deter toxicity will never end
An open mind with a creative spark that will continue to be stronger over time
I choose to follow my instincts; the soothing effect that soon comes like the sound of the heavenly bells that softly chime

I'd rather keep my plans tucked away in my own thoughts and not bear the option of letting others gain access to them
My mouth can either be my saving grace or a destructive weapon, but it's the energy from which it stems
The more happiness that I show, the more that misery struggles to flee
My good character shall not interfere with the presence of bad company

My life, my journey, my story
Every year distinguished as my chapter is narrated by me
I don't ever recall having to receive the approval of others to define my existence
For their solemn advice disguised as bitter hatred is non-existent

My state of mind is protected
I have walked away from peer reviews as they often became misconstrued
I bid farewell to vain, unhappy souls for in my life, their true colors are permanently ejected
I am in control of my own destiny and I have so much more to do

Broken Mirror

You pick and judge others based on assumptions
Somehow, you thought your own skeletons seemed to have rotted away
Please remind me when your life endured no scratches, no burns, no stains
As you perceive to live an easy life with no complaints

When your approach becomes one of egotism, you have already threw dirt
on your supposedly clean slate
Your wrongful mentality of mistreating others will deliver hurtful karma,
a devastating fate
As time permits, may you take the chance to humble yourself
For you will finally realize that perfection does not live in this world

I can see why it can be easier to judge on the outside instead of looking
from within
You're too comfortable looking through a broken mirror
Shattered, inaccurate pieces; experiencing the difficulty in seeing a flawed
reflection
Hopefully, you fix what was broken so you can see yourself much clearer

Think about this: the broken mirror prevents you from seeing yourself
completely but it can also symbolize your perfect image falling apart
Treat people right, they are more similar to you than you could ever imagine
You never know what they go through and where they have been
Let your conscience encourage you to be a helping hand to lend

I pray that you understand the severity of your words and actions
You are not superior over anyone
I can only imagine the speechless expression that is given
As your complete reflection will only reveal what you have assumed
everyone else to be, an imperfect character

A Life Not To Live

Don't ever assume
One day, it will all come back to you
Don't ever think you are better than anyone else
As you know you're not perfect
With this in mind, I hope you remain drenched in humility

Doubt and clouded sanity will only reel you into dying obscurity
Unhardened, unbreakable love will forever grant you lasting liberty
Always be fit to honor the matriarchs, patriarchs, and the one true God that shall remain first
They have gifted you with a legacy, gracefully kept and generationally preserved

You commit many wrongdoings but never hold yourself accountable
Haven't you learned the basis of karma?
Haven't you finally realized that it's time to grow up?
It's the season of change as you should desire to choose a prosperous, wholesome life instead of a bitter, ungrateful one, and that's a rhetorical dilemma

You should not emotionally detach yourself from the ones you love
You should not exist in moral disconnect but live in truth
You should not conform to the likeness of what others want you to be instead of what you were created to be
You should not be complacent in a life that tortures your mind and buries your soul

A life to influence
A life to freely invest compassion and empathy unto others
A life to share, a life to give
Sooner than later, real soon, will your life mirror what you were put on purpose in this world to do and to be

Blame

"The new kid did it"
"He doesn't know what he's doing"
"I have to explain this over and over for him to finally get it"
"He asks too many questions"
Forgive me, but I just started, please be patient with me

I thought some adults perfectly transitioned from the mindset of a child
I see that their swift temper tantrums and impatience proved otherwise
The frightening stare glued upon my face
A mature young man in the midst of grown adults who don't know how
and when to grow up is not only surprising, it's disturbing

I believe in myself
I know I have potential
I put my trust in the wrong people, the ones who didn't want to secure my
value
Here sits the déjà vu

I'm not afraid to admit my setbacks
It's rare to see the beauty of honesty
Lessons are learned as they make me better
No need to lie and maliciously cover my tracks
That's what manipulators do

I only hope they are provided the chance to see me today
Confident in my walk, easily adapted to growth
An epiphany inspired by tactless minds remaining blind to my obsession
with success
Unashamed of the blame, a narrow-minded game where the dishonest
choose to be unaccountable and end up perishing slowly

Micromanaged

Ever wonder why people watch every single thing you do
Through every aspect of your career, your education, and even your life
They could be jealous of where you're going; don't fret, you deserve it
They feel you're not good enough to be in the position that you're in; that's why you constantly prove them wrong
They want to live their own stagnant lives through you
Ignore the mess and let them see why you're so blessed

I know it's tiring as you've been through it all before
Yet be encouraged as you were able to step out of that revolving door, as the naysayers decided to keep spinning a little bit more
I love that you're glowing while the hearts and minds of others seem to be a bit sore
Therefore, your dignity was indeed exquisite in fighting for

Your growth is magnified as the negative opinions of others do not deter you from following your true calling
Take to heart Exodus 14:14—"Be still; The Lord will fight for you and you have only to be silent"
Seek your quiet place where you block out the unwanted noise
Be empowered as a flourishing model exemplifying the golden rule
Treat others the way you want to be treated as you're so much better than the ones who doubted you the very first time

Walking with a purpose, you stood tall
Focusing on yourself and giving your all
You never thought small
For others' stubbornness didn't make you fall

Attempted misfortunes granted you good fortune
The negative opinions surfaced around you granted you mercy
You see, you're too good for others to devour your journey only for them to conclude your success is not in vain
An ideal warrior that you are, you have survived what you been through and will thrive in what you will be

Can I

The alarming opinions that I would hear
It hurts, but please have the courage to come to me in person
Why do I allow myself to be validated by others?
Their facades are very convincing as their faces illuminate astonishment,
but their hearts hold on to jealousy

I listened and the words were hard to let go
Instead of relying on my own confidence, I babysat the nonsense of foolish
pride
It's my fault thinking they were proud supporters of mine but ended up
being two-faced foes
It's a shame their insecurities were too difficult to hide

Can I just be great?
For I know that I am a go-getter
Can I just do what's best for me?
For I shouldn't hold myself back to please others

Can I deserve better?
Can I give myself peace?
Can I not be happy?
Can I simply live?

Their words may have started to cut me, but they didn't permanently
bruise me
For I am realizing that I don't need permission from anyone to secure a
successful life
I'm moving on and I'm strong enough to do so
Their words have also empowered me and the surprising expressions that
they will show when they are proven wrong will be worthwhile

No Substance

Why be so hypocritical?
Judging the mishaps of others but never find fault in your own reflection
How I wish that personal lives will not be publicly advertised, the day we all
wait for this undisclosed miracle
Maybe it will be understood that placing tender care in our own lives will
move us in the right direction

So much disdain, people hiding behind a mask comfortably, which seems
to be their primary domain
Secrets to be kept have no issue of being breached
Leading with the misconception of a perfect life where there is no sight of
rain
Yet you trying to preach, but you seldom teach and reach

Blinded by the disgusted slander and libel
Obscured vision in recognizing your own skeletons
Before you aim your senseless feelings to hurt and devour, read your Holy
Bible
Give yourself a second chance to be redeemed again

Your negative actions induces complicated reactions
How you supposed to bind in spiritual health but have a materialistic spirit?
A disgrace to be involved in a pompous and negatively conscious faction
Where integrity and sympathy unevenly split

I pray you find displeasure in welcoming unhealthy distractions
Open your eyes to seize the chance to put spiteful things behind you
The stress and lack of energy that you consumed should hopefully fade
away like the pain of contractions
Therefore, I hope that the people you hurt will forgive you too

Enough

I refuse to be labeled as soft or overly sensitive
Why do people constantly mistake a good heart for a weak mind?
It is very rare these days to be someone who has so much to give
Even more so be a genuinely good person which can be so difficult to find

I refuse to be slandered as naïve
For my objective is to see the good in people
I remain sickened with evil dwelling in the arms of tranquility as I press for it to permanently leave
We have to elevate one another instead of the lying and chastising that is openly conceived

I refuse to be a punching bag
Belittled and battered with harsh words and reckless feelings
Yes, I am kindhearted and calm-natured but at the sight of malicious intent, I gladly gag
How much of one's immaturity is so long-term that it deteriorates the mindset of a victim needing imminent healing

The time will come when the spirit of discernment overflows
People will being to realize that strength and intolerability have leveled my backbone
Flesh attempted to bound me but I gradually fought it off by repeatedly saying no
I do not apologize if I disappoint you for your opinions of me I no longer loan

Chained with my passive thoughts, I broke free
I am enough but I've had enough with ignorant bliss
My life is bigger than one's insecurities and I am so proud that I can finally breathe
The new me is now embraced and the stress that once overtook me I do not miss

Child, Why Are You Weeping?

Crushed into pieces, sewn back together
Brushed aggressively in the fire, showered by the pouring rain
Confined to regrets, diligent in moving on
Child, the Lord gave you grace

Overlooked and misunderstood, praised for your vulnerability
Inaccurately judged, settling rumors
Contemplated suicide, being loved
Child, the Lord knew you had to be kept

Drowned in desperation, lifted in hope
Knocked unconsciously into your forgotten past
Only to awaken to the promised future that you had envisioned
Erased into obscurity, sketched in remembrance
Child, the Lord had great plans for you

Driven to the ground, placed back on your feet
Deserted by so-called companions, supported by strangers
Couldn't bear the thought of anybody to turn to
Yet one comes to mind who is always there
Child, the Lord will never leave you alone
It's time to smile again
Every obstacle caused a revelation that has wiped your tears away
Remember to pray and not doubt
For the Lord will work everything out

Anyday

Hands clasped tightly, closed eyes with purpose, heads arched downward praying that our home will soon be a better place

The selflessness, kindness, and respect that we had for one another has become very minimal these days, sometimes too barren to trace

How we anxiously wait in flooded tears, for the hour when divisiveness will weaken anyday

I'm at a loss for words . . . I just don't know what to say

Midnight

Today defeated me; I lost this battle
Loss after loss, failure after failure, I feel dead inside, completely damaged
My soul has been shaken aggressively to its core like a useless rattle
This day I can't seem to let go, vigorously haunting me, preparing me to become bitter and aged

What am I supposed to do? Please, self, enlighten me
I can't grace myself or anyone with a sweet smile, a heartfelt conversation, or a gentle laugh
I'm losing myself, mentally and spiritually
Chaotic unrest my spirit quickly lies in as my life is not precisely whole but devastatingly cut in half

My mind striking at a piercing tension
How I just itch to be calm and settled in a place encompassed with sheer delight
As I resort to cry and pray, my lips are eager to speak this day into an honorable mention
May my heart experience tranquil freedom as I close my eyes at midnight

A new day has arise and here I stand feeling completely different than the day before
My mindset switched from uncontrollable fear to unquestionable resilience
This day that altered my perception of being in control of all things is behind me and I can focus on myself even more
I can smile, talk, laugh, envision, and not dissipate into unbearable silence

I stress the importance of spiritual and mental release as I am no longer held captive to an unapologetic nightmare

An urgent scare provoking greater transparency when a speechless day inhibits agitated self-care

I have detached myself from the demonic pressure that occupied me in what I believed was a strenuous fight

All because I rested at midnight

Soldiers Handcrafted By God

Created to face overwhelming challenges yet remain resilient
Embedded with such a distinct fulfillment of strength and grace
Emptied of moral disfunction and filled with divine peace as one kneels towards a cry of repent
Bruised and battered by the heavy lows in this life but always rise proudly with pleasant smiles situated on our faces

Our strengths and weaknesses intertwined as one
Disheartened by the strains of life yet captivated by the willingness to move on and never give up
While enduring through some harsh trials, walking confidently with our heads held high should be all said and done
Self-value placed above harmful doubt should continually be embraced second to none

Molded gracefully from crystal dust
Perfectly made whole
Painted to reflect images of truth and serenity furnished through the rust
Destined to live a gracious life in spite of our imperfections shall be valued as our end goal

Through tears of sorrow, we are still wonderfully made
Through constant defeat, we are built to regain power
Through perfect position in God's will, our sincere faith will never fade
As long as time permits, we will finish the course on this Earth as fearless human beings in the final hour

We did not come this far to remain discouraged within our disappointments
For every battle that we won, God has truly blessed us to never enable our shining light to dim
Only what we do with a positive mindset and a generous attitude will bring forth much contentment
Being created with a divine purpose, we have been symbolically and beautifully handcrafted by him

One

For all of God's children inhabited among this world, we are all one
Skin color, nationality, religion; divinely being human is our main depiction
Some lust behind the notion of being superior, thrusting meaningless
actions and spewing hostility, ultimately leaving broken hearts undone
As we wish to face the reality of a perfect fairytale, this life that was given
to us all is far from fiction

A melting pot of beautiful creations
Welcomed to care for each other for dust we will pass away in
How I pray strong faith and unified courage will alleviate the hurt of a
crooked nation
We all bleed the same, but live in a country with such a tainted name

Division steered through prejudice, racism, and injustice
The difficulty of coming together when we steadily drift so far apart
Equality and fairness, the pillars of justice
Too many years wasted to get it right but now is the perfect time to start

Come what may
The pursuit of the heart freeing love
An open environment where no separation will refrain us to lay
Where we can all fly together in peace like beautiful white doves

We are all one
Never disconnected
Face the reality
Our souls do intersect

I Am, You Are

Let it be forever when we encourage one another and not just in the moment
We all have been placed in this world for a unique reason
Why does jealousy and competitive pressure even exist?
It is mandatory to support and acknowledge the emotional drive of one another as deception continues to linger in the midst

We're not meant to stay here for long
Therefore, it is necessary for all of us to get along
The anger that needs to be held back
The love that shall be forbidden to slack

Life is too short but too valuable to waste
Consider the precious moments that won't be taken into excessive haste for they will soon be unforgettable memories
Evil enjoys the sight of all of us tearing each other down
May it drown in the sea of togetherness as we strive to compliment one another

I am content, you are complete
I am kind, you are respected
I am intelligent, you are a visionary
I am everything, you are everything

Let me repeat this:

I am content, you are complete
I am kind, you are respected
I am intelligent, you are a visionary
I am everything, you are everything

Take this to heart
We need each other, we are one and the same, know your part
We're here to unify, motivate, and honor as we all have to leave from this world one day
To care for each other and to preserve positive minds and healthy lives will be the most integral way

Speak Up

You've been quiet for too long
Suffering each day holding everything in
You have a voice
Make use of it

Created to stand out, not to follow
Let others know where you stand
Show that you have dignity
For self-respect carries you much further than excessive flattery

When heavy problems arise, know how to withstand them in order to successfully bring them into closure
Just as Jesus exclaimed, "Peace Be Still", to calm the raging storm
You have the power to silence your own storm
Only then will your confidence to speak up will form

You've fought your battles long enough
Your emotions have been bottled up for so long
Your mind constantly replayed the times you've been used and tore down, all because you didn't see value in your voice
Seize the need to speak up to release your troubled soul

Establishing your independence instead of basking in the shadows of others
Standing firm in your honest truth
Simply accepting the benefit of being heard
You will no longer remain in silence as your voice will be impactful in moving mountains

The Outcast

The loner
The quiet one
The awkward one
The one that can't be figured out

I was labeled as a nerd just because I used my brain a lot more
Teased for being unaesthetic to plenty
Targeted due to my calm, reserved nature
Through it all, I was protected through self-love as I was too proud and too bold to ever fit in

Middle school and high school brought some trying times for some
Hormones raging, puberty in full effect
Easily obliged to peer pressure, knowing that it interfered with the morals and values that were taught
Leaving good friends behind to blend in with the wrong crowd, only for reality to announce that you need them again

I didn't need to impress anyone
For I am here to please the Lord himself
I've always been pushed to live my life on my own standards
Not from the thoughts of anyone else

An honorable life I chose to settle in
How frustrating it must be to follow behind the shadows of others
I would rather view myself as an outcast instead of a people-pleaser
Spontaneous and generous I will continue to be, inconsistent and shifty I will always frown upon

Tree Of Life

God is so great to have created a symbol of strength that represents the evident beauty of nature
The resilient tree that holds unique aspects to make it whole:

- The branches
- The leaves
- The roots

How amazing it is for our lives to correlate with the essence of the tree adapted to be so firm

The branches are what I claim to be the glue
They hold the leaves (our decisions) together where they can help express our beauty and make us who we are
They tighten their grips when the rushing wind attempts to pull us into independence too soon
In due time, some may break due to weariness but it's the branches that remain attached that keep us in line

The leaves are what I claim to be the masterpiece
They represent our overall character
They feed into experience, as our decisions and flaws influence us to acquire maturity
It's also clear that some leaves do wilt, fall off, and pass away, which represents our bad decisions and scars being buried behind us

The roots are what I claim to be the foundation
They hold true to being the forefront, keeping everything in perfect shape
Easy to withstand, difficult to tear away
When the tree begins to lean, it's the roots that straighten it to where it originally stood

The tree of life
A majestic force of nature
On solid ground where it shall never be moved
On uninterrupted land where it shall forever stand

Positive Fruit

A healthy tree bears great fruit
Love heals
Authenticity creates
Empathy fulfills

Selfless leadership empowers
Poignant grace inspires
Inner confidence transcends
Complete strength prevails

Sympathy soothes the urge to grieve
Kindness changes the evil blueprint that this cruel world was determined
to leave
Hope enlightens adequate progress towards a grateful destiny
Faith truly unlocks the riveting potential for where one needs to go and
needs to be

Respect blushes to integrity
Joy resents to the turmoil of pain
Maturity turns its slick back to corrupt behavior
Wisdom remains the catalyst to the journeys of those rich in growth

Vital happiness symbolized by the beaming sunshine
Unity we all should bleed
Laughter that refreshes the soul
The positive fruit that nurtures a divine temple

Thank You Mom and Dad

To my beautiful mother, my main encourager
To my humble father, my main inspiration
Through your intercessory prayer and gracious support, my spirit was always uplifted, never discouraged
Your endless love and comforting wisdom will seldom fade and remain still in my heart for a lasting duration

You raised me to cherish the spiritual fulfillment of Christ Jesus, along with my tenacious siblings
Wrapped me with unparalleled fortitude in order to endure through the harshest trials
Compassion and faith . . . acquired assets that benefit what a glorious life brings
Being my absolute best stems from your sound advice and how much you sacrificed with the extra mile

Mom, you inspire precocious children with your gifted abilities of teaching and nurturing
Dad, you guide spiritually-grounded believers towards salvation
What more could I have of a strong-minded, sharp-tongued, patient, and understanding queen and king
Obedience and morality resulting in the betterment of mankind, the equation helping to evoke a healthy conversation

Your tough love and open transparency enables me to realize there's no such thing as perfection
I feel much better knowing that through all of my mistakes, you still love me
Please do know that your willingness to direct me on the right path as well as helping others will forever be recognized
When in doubt, you push me to pursue my limitless dreams once thought imaginary

We celebrate the both of you
To my mother, you will never be compared to another
To my father, your presence as a natural-born leader inspires your two sons and one daughter
Carrying out both of your legacies is what we will intend to do

As each day passes by, we are reminded
As the both of you grow older, we honor
We laugh, cry, and engage when sudden memories play into rewind
Mom and Dad, thank you for simply being you and we thank the Good Lord for the blessings that he has in store

Wishing You Well

The storm is passing over
You've been entrapped in your feelings of brokenness and guilt
Fear and struggle lured you into being a lost cause
With the premature effect of a dimmed life unfortunately built

The day has come
You have encountered your greatest blessing
Now free from desperation, you are equipped for greatness
How beautiful it is to accept change for such a defeated spirit

A soul now made whole
As you have settled in strength
A life that once disappeared within the darkness
Your light now gleams so brightly that it will shine forever

Remember to look at yourself in the mirror
Be vigilant of the tapped potential that's been longing to exist
You are a gift
You are enough

Your future remains in your hands
The daylight unapologetically basks upon your face
Overwhelming peace that you are fully covered in
You are a living testimony of significant growth

A Lifelong Dream (Intro)

This specific poem is a special one that I intended to save for last. The significant meaning behind this poem lies from a soldier who exemplified extraordinary resilience, unmasked courage, lasting faith, sound integrity, wholesome gratitude, and impeccable confidence. This impactful human being is known as Jesse Owens. A selfless man who had to endure and persevere through harsh obstacles to become an influential force to be reckoned with in the versatile sport of track and field. Not only was Jesse successful in achieving his aspirations but he was one of many who broke barriers for African-Americans, both male and female, to reflect their own history in being renowned track and field athletes. In terms of the immaculate legacy that he had left behind, it was realized that Jesse approached divine peace in the midst of his own storm as he faced his share of racism, disrespect, and negativity while preparing for and competing in the 1936 Berlin Olympics. However, with the tenacity, hope, purpose, and worth that he embraced within himself, he was able to move forward from the background noise and receive four gold medals in a city where he was heavily disliked, specifically from its dictator during that time.

This poem also resonates with me because of not only symbolizing the overall theme of this book but because this was my very first poem that I wrote when I was twelve years old, during my time in the 7th grade. While I also had the option of writing an essay or doing a collage, this was something I knew in my heart I could set forth to do as I saw fit in capturing his essence through the powerful and stirring concept of poetry. As the poem was reflected upon once more, I wanted to preserve its authenticity that was placed into it when I first wrote it. I also want to mention that it is amazing how my very first poem has come around full-circle in helping to represent my debut poetry collection. Therefore, it was with my distinct pleasure that I present to you, A Lifelong Dream.

A Lifelong Dream

It all started when this great child of God was born into his mother's hands
At the age of five, his mother torn open his chest to take a huge bump out so
he wouldn't experience any concussions and growth defects
Even though his family was poor to see a doctor, his mother still had the
faith and the courage to do what was needed for the bump to be removed
He cried like a loud horn until the treatment was over
The sigh of relief his father felt as soon as he became calm

Jesse worked in cotton fields, picking up hundreds of cotton
He took care of his four sisters and four brothers until the tragic, untimely
death of his adult sister
So you're probably wondering why did his mother have that many children?
It's in the heart of being a Christian, teaching her children what's right and
reading the Bible, so they can walk into their future that will shine very bright

In high school, a young man arrived, very athletic and very gifted
Each time he ran, he went faster
He didn't need a fan
All he needed was good hydration and a new coach
Thank goodness for change as his coach taught him everything he needed
to know, especially when he earned his medals

"Kolledge" (college) happened for him as well
Winning track meets with gifted speed and endurance
He married his college sweetheart and also practiced everyday for the
Olympics so Adolf Hitler wouldn't get in his way
Many German athletes adored him and how pleasurable it was when they
liked you for who you were

Jesse, we all know that you died of lung cancer but we are pleased with the fine legacy that you have left behind
The people you knew and loved will always remember you as a dove of peace
Your family and friends will forever honor you as their lifelong dream

In Memory of Jesse Owens: A Life of Endurance
(September 12, 1913—March 31, 1980)

www.ingramcontent.com/pod-product-compliance
Lightning Source LLC
LaVergne TN
LVHW051706080426
835511LV00017B/2754